ginny findlow

Faith

Is an

Act of Will

Front cover: Summer House at Caesarea
Who is the more vulnerable? This lady or
The Jew in the high-rise apartment.

Also by same author

In the Beginning there was Trust

English 2009

[Arabic and Hebrew 2010]

ISBN 978-1-4466-2523-1

Contents

1 Universal Presence of ‘Dhimmitude’

2 Domestic Violence & the Battered Wife

3 Universal Influence of Depression

4 Far-reaching Consequences

5 Universal Influence of Media

6 Different View of Israel

7 The Combatants

8 Family Counselling View of the Conflict

9 How the Family Metaphor Helps

10 The [Full] Process

Preface

The Fourth Option – FAITH

Welcome to this simple book that questions the recent arguments against Islam that are used as a basis for rejection of Muslim claims to land in Palestine. My attitude is simple and practical, and gets away [I hope] from complicated comparative scripture analysis and long-standing prejudice. The attitude is based on theory used in family counselling, which aims to get family members to hear one another accurately and respond to heart-felt needs. It assumes that there is enough goodness in individuals, no matter how angry or upset, to respond to the [Universal] Spirit, releasing motivation for resolution of conflict, and adoption of new ways of behaving toward one another.

In the last analysis, the **key to resolution is an act of will**: The decision to have faith in the process, in the individuals enabling the process, in the folk 'on the other side' and in FAITH ITSELF [Allah/God.].]

The other 'three options' alluded to are **conversion**, [replacement theology] **death** [by suicide or war,] or a grudging tolerance [poorly disguised **hatred**] that makes the person subservient [what we have now.] They are **not really options at all** in 2011.

Universal Presence of Dhimmitude

General global response to Muslims since 9/11 seems to be divided into two camps: one positive and welcoming [labelled 'politically correct' by their opponents] and the other negative and fear-based [labelled racist, islamophobic by their opponents. Those who are frightened by the terror and its link with the Koran, are quick to point out the human rights failings of Islamist States such as Iran and Saudi Arabia and to impose these onto the character of the vast majority of Muslims else-where. All this in spite of quite different scenarios to be found in Indonesia and Turkey for example. [That is not to say that human rights violations do not occur - Coptic Christians do occupy an inferior role on the rubbish dumps of Cairo it's true and the too-familiar long-standing injustices such as these **do** need attention.]

Human Rights & The Church

When we look closer at Western society it isn't very long since the U.N. had to attend to the unconditional equality of human beings, legislating for human rights. This attention *preceded* that of the Church which has been very slow to understand the nature of the vertical relationship between Jesus and the Father, and the vertical relationship between an individual Christian and God. The Church [especially the Roman Catholic Church] has always envisaged these relationships to be hierarchical, and the Anglican church's deacon/priest/bishop scheme is seen in the same light. Sydney Anglicans still believe that the husband is the head of the family, and elsewhere the celebrant at Holy Communion is considered to be more elevated than the recipient. Up until the charismatic renewal at the end of the 20th C no-one had ever even *thought* about the *horizontal* relationships between members of the congregation being important.

Past Mistakes by Government

In Australia we are still suffering the emotional fall-out from aborigines who were in Missions in the Torres Straight Islands, Queensland and the Northern Territories. Their hatred of white Australians is still strong although the officials who acted it out have long gone. Prime Minister Kevin Rudd apologised to the 'stolen generation' but there is still a lot more work to be done. It is not long since apartheid was abolished in South Africa through Nelson Mandela, or Black Americans were liberated through Martin Luther King. Women are **still** expected to sit at the back of the bus in Israel and non-Jewish women can still remember being spat on by fundamentalist Jews for walking [as a child] through their area of Jerusalem wearing short sleeves. Is it so surprising that un-reformed Islam of the 14th C still displays the unpleasant aspect of dhimmitude, brought to our attention recently by folk such as Dr Wafa Sultan [ex-Syrian psychiatrist] and Marcel Rebiai [Algerian Christian-adopted evangelical pastor.] Dr Mark Durie rector of Caulfield Anglican Church has also written a book called 'The 3rd choice', which refers to the fate of the non-Muslim in an Islamist-conquered land. [The other 2 choices are death and conversion.]

20th Century Racism by 'western' powers.

The concepts of imperialism and colonialism have been done to death already, [the British Empire being the most constant foil] exposing the hierarchical and exploitative relationship between indigenous and coloniser; both it and its corollary racism were alive and well in Australia around Federation [Melanesians originally imported to work in the Queensland sugar-cane industry were then all sent home] and after Federation the immigration of Chinese was limited [1906]. The 'keep Australia white' policy was active from **1890 right up to the 1970's**, when Indo-Chinese were accepted. [Large-scale post-war immigration by ship had thus far mainly consisted of white Caucasians from Europe and Russia who were expected to assimilate via language and behaviour.]

Suffrage – international comparisons

Australian aborigines did not become full citizens until 1962, but **British women** did not get the vote in the United Kingdom until **1928**, shortly after they were allowed to join men in the Universities [mainly to watch and attend lectures, not to obtain equivalent degrees.] Henry 6th 1432 allowed only male owners of property [of a certain value] to vote. Over the next 580yrs those in power have doggedly sought ways of denying voting rights to folk with a different religious persuasion, [Protestant vs Catholic] social group, wealth, knowledge, residency, nationality etc from themselves. Only from 1867 were **all** male house-holders allowed to vote in the U.K. After WW1 [1918] women had to be over 30 and property-owners; it was only in 1928 that they became equal with men, from aged 21. [I've got the key of the door, never been 20-one before, my father says I can do as I like, so shout hip,hip, hooray, For he's a jolly good fellow, he's 20 -one today!]

A list of [Muslim] countries with dates when women obtained suffrage:

Turkey 1930. Indonesia 1945. British Palestine 1946. Lebanon 1952. Syria 1953. Egypt, 1956. Iran 1963

1999-2006 Qatar, Bahrein, Oman, Kuwait,UAE. **Saudi Arabia – none**

Australian women 1902/*Aboriginal* women 1962 Canadian women 1917/Canadian *Indian* women 1960.

Domestic Violence

Domestic violence [verbal and physical] occurs right across the world, in all cultures and across society, irrespective of economic status, and gender. The numbers are six times greater for women than for men, but men are less likely to report it when they are the victims. These 'domestic'violent crimes against women are usually perpetrated by boy-friends, husbands or ex-husbands. [Violent men react badly to loss of their partner, often stalking her – perhaps even for years – until they find and murder her. These terrible crimes happen just the same in **Western** civilised countries where the record of political human rights abuse is very low and there is no Islamic Law.

Domestic Violence & the Battered Wife

Hindu and Muslim activists have been fighting domestic violence in Kashmir together. Various studies in different countries have found that half of Palestinian women have been victims, and 80% of women surveyed in rural Egypt said they were beaten -often for refusing to have sex with their husbands. [In Egypt sexual harassment of Muslim women on the street is also very common.] In Pakistan 90% of women were subject to verbal, sexual, emotional or physical abuse, in the privacy of their own homes, and something like two-thirds of women in some of Nigeria's communities said they were victims. In Australia aboriginal women are 40 times as likely to suffer domestic violence as their white sisters. Psychology tells us that those countries where there is oppression by an occupying army will have correspondingly greater levels of domestic unrest [because the anger and frustration of the oppressed men is passed down to their families.] Obviously there is great upheaval in Pakistan at the moment as they contend with extreme nationalism and terrorism, as well as a war going on at its borders.

Does Islam cause it /make much difference

Islamic law has been criticized for promoting domestic violence by privileging males over females, [women are supposed to be chaste and modest while men are allowed to divorce at will and have several wives] but this is the same deal that operates in most societies even in the west– there is nothing particularly Muslim in this state of affairs. Part of the effect on immigrant Muslim women is the result of cultural ignorance, and manipulation by males who erroneously [but cunningly] cite the Koran as back-up. Naturally the Muslim wives want to stay faithful to their religion, so this can be used against them by socially embarrassed family members to pressure her to stay. As in all other places where abuse occurs, it is a cause for shame which leads to denial and cover-up – whether at the mosque, at the hospital or police station. But in their adopted western societies Imams are now beginning to speak out and teach Muslim women about their rights.

Some Imams hold counselling sessions for engaged couples, as well as for those married couples experiencing difficulties. A Washington area Imam said "For many years, our community did not face these issues. Women suffered in silence and fear. Even today, many imams think it could never happen in their mosque." "Islam gives equal rights to men and women, but there are myths in Muslim society that men are superior and violence is permitted. This is wrong, and it needs to be said." That idea has more to do with the chauvinism of Arab culture, than Islam.

As in other countries Imams and social workers in the U.S are trying to engage Muslim men to form groups 'Muslim Men Against Domestic Violence' but getting volunteers is not easy – which is just the same situation as amongst white communities in Australia or U.K. And when taken to court they come up with the same excuses. Muslim culture, with its tradition of arranged marriages where brides are sent to live with their in-laws, can see immigrant brides cut off from their families and isolated in new households, where they might be lowest in the pecking order and expected to act as servants. But the same situation can occur in geographically isolated western nuclear families [living where the work is] where there is no extended family to be aware of what is going on and stick up for the injured party.

There is no shortage of programs in developed countries to help Muslim women who are being abused, such as hotlines with links to Arabic speakers and shelters that serve halal meat but if they speak no English and are relying on their in-laws for help, they might just as well be living in a remote Moroccan village. Sometimes an abusive husband might threaten to "call immigration" and have the wife deported. Unfortunately some Muslim wives do not know that there are U.S. laws allowing them to seek alternate residency if they can prove they have been abused by their spouses, or that there are organisations who offer legal aid free of charge [for obtaining restraining orders and child custody.]

"Frequently women refuse the offer to go into shelters. Even if the man is beating her and the children, she may feel it is her Islamic duty to remain home and respect him," said one of the women's health workers. "We try to show them that in Islam, their rights are protected and their duty is only to God. When they finally understand, they are so relieved. It takes a lot of courage to decide to take action, and then to actually make the emergency call, but if/when she finally does, the police come in a patrol car and help her pack while the husband and in-laws watch in utter amazement." As a practising doctor/counsellor I have had the same experience with Australian victims. They can be brought right up to the point where they agree that making a break is the right thing to do. Then they go back on what they have decided, and go back home to the trauma. It's almost like giving up chocolate or following a diet – in the last analysis you can persuade yourself that if you resume your previous weight you are no worse off than you were before – and you coped **then**, didn't you?

Natural Resistance to Intervention & Family Break-up

Organizations that help women escape are often seen by conservative Muslims as sabotaging good Islamic family values, but Anglican and Catholic priests do exactly the same thing in England and Australia, perhaps less often now than they did in the past. Family members and friends will also sort themselves into 'for and against' with respect to her actions – just as they do after a divorce, compounding the emotional loss. Most often in western families it is simply the loss of self-esteem and the wearing down of volition that prevents a chronically victimised woman from accepting help – religious faith has nothing to do with it. In all cases the shame is paramount. The victim always believes it is *her* fault. [As do victims of sexual abuse.]

Original Evil [Who is **not** guilty?]

In all of these examples I have been illustrating the fact that extraction of dhimmitude is everywhere on the planet and ingrained in every-one, because it is the dark side of human nature [whatever you call it.] Since women have got equal rights in the west as a result of feminist activism, all that has happened is that women now drink, smoke and behave promiscuously to the same extent as men. There are now female gangs, and girls are as violent as teenage boys. In America [a matriarchal country] domestic violence is more commonly performed **by** women [the so-called gentler sex] **on** their men-folk.

The use of power in relationships is our **original** sin, it has always been with us.

The road out of sin and into equality [democracy and human rights do not come naturally – we have to work at it and legislate for it] is a hard one, as testified by people like Mandela and Luther-King, and the personal road is also arduous. But like Paul, we can say " by GRACE we are saved, and that not of ourselves – it is a gift from God." God offered it to **us** 'when we were yet sinners', and it was the offer and the gift received that changed us. So it is with the offer of friendship [and equality] that we make to the Muslims. It is a matter of faith. Either we think they are ordinary folk like ourselves, capable of responding *to* love *with* love, or we think they are some sort of aliens – different in the quality of their humanity and the extent of their potential. I'm pretty sure it is the former that more accurately represents the truth.

Extending Boundaries of Understanding

It is hardly surprising that the Koran is misunderstood and misrepresented, just as is the Bible. Even though the New Testament is there for all to see, there are still folk who don't 'get' the nature of unconditional love, and behave to their fellow-countrymen as though they are living in Moses' time, majoring in 'the law' and O.T. quotations, causing embarrassment to sensible Christians who are struggling to witness to the love of Christ. Many of the themes that are thought strange in the Koran have a parallel in the O.T. such as 'magic numbers' [40 days and 40 nights, meaning 'a long time' and 70 virgins as a prize for the martyr] or a parallel in western history such as the practice of 'winner takes all' i.e. the widow /family/possessions going to the victor of the last battle

Since the Koran involves revelation coming through only one man, it is difficult to convey concepts that talk about relationship. It is difficult to transmit in words the essence of 'islam,' the nature of willing submission of a man to God. You need at least **two** people to demonstrate mutual willing submission – as in a marriage of two people who love one another, or two members [brothers /sisters] in the mosque who care about one another. We started out with hierarchy [in Christianity] and are only just beginning to understand Jesus when he said to his disciples 'I have called you friends.' We have never understood the servant-hood relationship properly – we changed it into duty and compulsion. Why should we, then, expect Muslims to be any further ahead than we are? - when the Koran was written 1300 yrs ago, capturing culture at one concrete time in history. [Especially as the East has not had the benefit of self-examination and critical thinking that was afforded to the west by the enlightenment.] As in the Bible there are some central things that must/do endure over time; but there are others less important that apply to *specific* circumstances, that inevitably change over the centuries.

Rejection of Tit for Tat Theology

Durie notes in 'The third Option' that many of Islamic *dhimma* rules may have had **Byzantine** origins and were later adopted by the **Norman** conquerors of Arab occupied Sicily (in a kind of reverse dhimmi-tude). There were also **Spanish** adaptations of the *jizyah* following the Reconquista of Muslim occupied Andalusia in which they extracted *tributo* from the conquered Muslims. [Jizyah was the annual ceremony where the non-muslim was reminded of his relative servitude and indebtedness to his local government.] Just as the ancient 'eye-for-an-eye' system ensured that the enmity was prolonged indefinitely, *we must just as firmly reject the notion that present-day Muslims are helplessly imprisoned in the persona of their 14th C ancestors, and incapable of rising to the 21st C occasion* of living harmoniously with the west. It would be tragic if our own fear and rejection became **the** imprisoning force, acting to bring about the very events that terrify us most.

The question is not about the relative merits of three holy books. It is not about whether WE can relate to the negative stuff in the Koran, [that most Muslims gloss over and hardly notice, compared with the good bits they use all the time.] [We do exactly the same with the gory parts of the O.T. having learned to 'eat the meat, and leave the bones at the side of the plate.'] The question is "What does the Koran mean to its Muslim devotees?" "Can **they** live with it?" And most important of all, "can we relate to **these people**?" It's not our job to criticise their holy book, [or vice versa.] Both groups of people have a responsibility to act as stewards for their own scriptures.

Two news items encourage me today. One showed a member of a mosque in Luton agonising over whether he had failed the car bomber [Sweden] by making public this man's violent tendency -which resulted in his leaving the mosque, going to Sweden and organising a plot [that failed.] The love in the face and words of that Muslim on TV was beautiful to see. The second piece of news was the arrest of Bakar Bashir in Indonesia, the old man who supported the terrorists who caused the Bali bombing. All this time the Indonesian police had been working to assemble sufficient evidence to convict him, especially when they discovered a training camp in March this year. It is reassuring to be reminded that those who are involved as terrorists are a very small minority [and that Muslim governments are working hard to keep them in check.]

Universal Influence of Depression

There is so much room for compassion in the bigger story [the fight for Jerusalem and the land of Palestine.] Both sides have suffered, and are suffering, now.

When the Muslims see the wonderful Dome of the Rock in all its splendour the pride is bittersweet, harking back to a time when the people had good governance and there were signs every day that Allah was with them. They could be forgiven today for thinking He had forgotten them. The oil riches have stayed in the hands of the already rich, who curry favour with the west by displaying their wealth and sophistication [in comparison with their un-educated and under-privileged masses.] There is no sharing [no 'common-wealth'] and few signs that things will change.

Muslims traditionally are not people who lie down and take a kicking without responding to defend themselves. Even so, it was only when they had reached extreme levels of diminishment that activists took matters into their own hands in the 50's and 60's. Osama bin Laden has driven the protest in a previously un-imaginable, horrendous direction, but few would argue that there is nothing to protest.

So by the active expression of their anger [against those they feel are to blame] the Muslim terrorists act out their frustration and pain. Against 'the enemy'. The Jews however have a different way of expressing their grief. They turn the anger onto themselves, and they become de-pressed. For example, the Muslims had a blank slate to work with, a big empty area where the temple had stood. But they didn't attach themselves to the part left standing in situ – [the wailing wall] – or take any particular notice of it. The temple[s] had **gone** = <u>fact of life.</u> They built another one, equally beautiful to enclose/protect and venerate the most important part of it [for which we all owe a debt of gratitude to Abd al-Malik.]

Let's look at the words chanted at the wailing wall. Colin Thubron says that on festivals, and the anniversary of the temple's fall,

'the whisper of the faithful swells to a heart-rending roar.'

"For the palace that lies desolate," cries one
"*We sit in solitude and mourn,*" the chorus answers.
"For the walls that are overthrown,
We sit in solitude and mourn.
For our glory which is departed,
For our wise men who have perished,
For the priests who have stumbled,
For our kings who have despised Him,.........
We sit in solitude and mourn."

This is a list of emotional losses incurred by the demise of The Temple:

1.desolate palace – our own ruler has been usurped by another

2.over thrown walls – our defences were not effective, our boundaries were transgressed.

3.departed glory – more than just self-esteem: the jealousy, admiration, approval of the world has gone.

4. our wise men perished – loss of human resource + goodness destroyed

5. stumbling priests – we have been led astray, [*they* sinned, *we* suffer]

6. Kings despising God's Law – *they* have let us down, *we* get the pain.

The first 3 refer to MY personal loss/pain, number 4 to loss of goodness [i.e.God's loss] and the last 2 to the unfairness of a situation where I suffer as a result of other folks' actions.

The response to ALL of them is to sit, be isolated, mourn.

Applying the above to the Domestic Violence scenario, which is usually chronic;

1. Some-one else's will is in charge. [I am not master of my own life]
2. My person-hood has been violated/boundary crossed. My defences are useless.
3. I am miserable, ugly, pathetic, no-one could like me
4. I will never be loving again – I am ruined for ever
5. That's what you get for marrying a mummy's boy. It's my fault
6. I know he does wrong but I know he doesn't mean it. He cant help it, he has so much on his mind & he loses it. It's my fault.

Sitting is what you do when you have no energy. [Loss of movement /loss of activity associated with depression.]

Solitude is what you seek when you are injured mentally, you want to be left alone, feel alienated from others.

Mourning is what you do when you have just experienced a huge loss, something or somebody very significant in your life.

The normal mourning or grief reaction is a way of healing and getting back to normal, [and usually eastern cultures do a much better job than us westerners] but sometimes there are a series of losses – one after the other, and the grief becomes a chronic state. Alternatively a patient can *choose* to stay in the grieving state for various psychological reasons. [She has not made a *conscious* choice; in fact she is confused about why she is not getting better.]

In Australia the percentage of the population who have the genetic make-up for the personality pre-disposed to depression is about 12 ½%, that is half of a half of a half =1/8. The percentage of the Jewish population might be much higher – perhaps even 50% - because of the cultural separation maintained over millennia. Because of the global repercussions of Jewish history it is quite likely that there are comparative studies available of the predisposing genetics: how it relates to variations in rates of depression across cultures. It would be interesting to have this information.

Note: said info is in, see bibliography for research articles and psychiatry. Best book – Inside the Jewish Mind by Raphael Patai, a cultural anthropologist/Rabbi.

Far-reaching Consequences

Everyone knows that fellowship [sharing of selves] is what life's about. Two people who are old friends [fellowship together] may be of differing races, cultures and so on – even on opposite 'sides' in a war. Romeo and Juliet belonged to warring families, the English royal family was divided by the first world war, Nazis and allied soldiers called a Christmas truce and fellowshipped together then resumed "what they were sent there to do" [i.e. kill one another] the next day.

My psychiatric research has proved what I suspected – also what the near-eastern Arabs already knew in 1947 when they reacted against the idea of Jewish immigrants returning to Israel. They had been used to living alongside Jews for centuries. Nobody in Jerusalem much cared where you were from, they all mucked in together. But they suspected [and they were right] that the western Jews were different.

Eastern philosophy – possibly because of the heat? – has always been to do with just 'BEING' [in the present] and western philosophy has had more to do with 'achieving', being busy, getting things done. The British were considered to be quite silly when they followed the same routines that worked at home, regardless of the stifling heat. Hence Noel Coward's song "Mad dogs and Englishmen go out in the noon-day sun!" My research showed that Eastern Jews and Eastern Arabs have similar personality structure, but there is a difference between Eastern and Western Jews.

Just as Darwin found with his island species, when animals are isolated by geography for a long time from the parent group [as the western Diaspora have been removed from the Levant] they undergo gradual changes which may not be noticed by themselves, but when compared with original animals in the parent group exhibit definite new characteristics. The Arabs were shrewd enough to realise that the Jews who wanted to immigrate back to Palestine were not the same people who had lived quietly side by side with other nationalities in the past, just one among equals. These folk wanted to be in charge. [They didn't want just 'to be', they wanted to make changes and transform the land into 'their own.'] Arabs knew that the Jews coming back to home base would not 'fit in,' because without knowing it they had changed: they had become western.

This brings up the basic question that existed when I was a child [1943] in England, and there was still a 'colour bar'. Even if you had no prejudice yourself, should one purposely challenge the colour bar by marrying the opposite 'colour', knowing that it would cause problems in every direction, or did one avoid trouble by seeking friendship amongst your own? Should we try to avoid future trouble where it is clearly evident, or should we accept the situation/trouble and work through it? I think this was the situation being resisted in 1947, not the fact that the Jews wanted "only 18% of the land." It was the 'foot-in-the-door' or the wedge, that everyone could see was just the beginning of the end.

Once the Jewish immigrants were back [with persecution fresh in their minds] they became consciously aware of *their* difference and the different *surroundings* – weather, topography neighbours etc. First of all is the recognition "I feel different, I *am* different." [Muslims and Eastern Jews *are* different, in many respects, from Western Jews as we said earlier.] Next comes the strange bit; as a psychological defence against something being wrong with ME, it changes round in my head to 'there is something wrong with THEM – THEY are different." [=not normal, queer, odd.]

One of the commonest ways of coping with strangeness of another people eg Native Indians in USA, aborigines in Australia, Arabs and assorted nationalities in Palestine, Africans in S.Africa , was to round them up and take them round the corner somewhere so you couldn't see them. Out of sight, out of mind! [That was the theory , but it didn't work.] The strategy is a form of denial.

The facts are: I cannot **change** you into somebody I could like, I cannot **kill** you because somebody would notice, I can't **live with you** as you are. I have a big problem. What shall I do? Take them away somewhere *so I am not reminded* of my problem! Separate the two groups so they can live two separate lives. Apart-ness, Apartheid. Because the ancient [biblical] culture of Israel from Abraham onwards was based on cultural separation [for a special purpose, and for a limited time] it is easy to see how this idea would present itself as a solution.

If you draw any kind of line to separate people into two camps – the acceptable and the rejects, the ones labelled 'rejects' will *become* your enemy – even if they were not enemies before. People who are rejected, denied rights and privileges will become angry and become enemies. The 410 km defensive concrete wall works in such a way, the check-points between separate living areas works in this way. All of it works to make enemies, not friends. And it started with feeling awkward and uncomfortable "in a strange land" that *ought* to have felt like paradise!

I am pretty sure that the Jewish folk fleeing after WW2 would have felt strange and dissatisfied no matter where they were – in any country of the world – even in heaven itself. The damage was inside them, they took it with them wherever they went. Eastern Jews however were embedded in their lands. "We have always been here." Like Eastern Arabs they have a strong sense of belonging and purpose, = identity. Those returning have been displaced, they have a different identity, to do with loss ['home-sickness'] just like the exiles in Babylon and the battered wives. **Starting with the solitude** of grief and mourning, they **have acted to bring about even more** separation and loneliness.

What are the seven features of the battered wife? If we go back to chapter 3 we find some conclusions that battered wives make about the world. They are different from the conclusions that normal emotionally healthy individuals make, but these conclusions **ARE TRUE for the individuals who have had** these experiences. That is, **until** they have had experiences which prove otherwise.

1. I am not master of my own life.

   Hopeless, incompetent, can't do anything right. I'll have to TRY MUCH HARDER to gain control of the situation.

   *No. **Dont try harder**, change direction. **Try less** of the control, and more of the good neighbour.*

2. My defences are useless

   I'll have to make them MUCH bigger & more secure/?nuclear.

   *No. Your **best defence** is to be a **good neighbour**.*

3. No-one could like me

   Everybody hates me – especially Arabs & Muslims. There's nothing I can do to change it. [Not after 2000yrs history.]

   *Not true. When you are not threatened you are very attractive, intelligent and funny. Plus - There is **LOTS you can do**.*

4. I am ruined for ever

   I will never have a happy life, I am doomed to chronic despair.

   *That's rubbish! Don't be so dramatic. You **could** have a life – just **decide** to HAVE FAITH that **it is possible**.*

5. . It's my fault

We shouldn't have disagreed with the UN and acted alone.

*True, **we started it.** We even performed the first terrorist act. [Blew up St David's Hotel.]*

6. . It's my fault.

I suppose if we assassinate their leaders, they will reply with violence. *[True, but **they** are responsible for **their** violence, as I am for **mine**.]*

The domestic violence analogy is not absolutely fool-proof. *E.g.number 5 – I married him - is true, [although he may not have displayed his violent nature when she made that decision.] but number 6 –" I burned the dinner, therefore he is justified in hitting me" is not. Also number 1- she would try harder "to gain his approval," whereas Israel tries harder to get on top of it by being MORE violent/more controlling.*

Universal Influence of the Media

Re : Re: Arab woman asks Arab men to rape Israeli girls!!!

« **Reply #8 on:** January 10, 2009, 11:33:23 AM »

Peace,

She's not asking Arab men to rape Israeli women, at all. She flatly denied wanting that. She said she's not asking for Arab men to rape Israeli women and she doesn't think it will come to that because the Arab resistance has much higher morals than that [according to her at least], and hence wouldn't start raping anyone. But she does say, that if that did happen [she's giving a hypothetical although it is still pretty misguided in my opinion], that Israeli women who are raped [or harassed for that matter] should not have any rights under the laws in Arab countries [specifically Egypt I suppose], but should just leave those Arab countries if they don't want to be raped. So she's not encouraging Arab men to rape Israeli women. She's encouraging Arab men to sexually harass Israeli women in Arab countries as a way to get them to leave Arab countries. She said that her whole point was that she wants to see Israeli Zionist women OUT of Arab countries, and if sexual harassment, which Arab men already do to other Arab women, will help that goal then it should be encouraged.

I don't agree with her, but that is what she said. She's not encouraging rape, JUST sexual harassment as a form of harrassment to push Israeli Zionists out of her country. I definitely think this woman is a weirdo, but I also think it's funny how this video was posted knowing that westerners equate sexual harassment with rape [taboo buzz words] especially if they fall in the same sentence, and will be disgusted by how this is seriously being talked about on a news channel and think that this represents Arab culture as a whole and that even the women believe in this kind of stuff, instead of understanding the context and concluding that this woman is just plain old wierd. She sees sexual harassment as something totally inappropriate and on the level of any kind of harassment, which should not be applied to good people but people who she considers as evil [Israeli Zionists in particular] should not be seen or treated as good people should be treated, and should be harassed without recourse for them because they are evil. Hence she thinks it's okay to harass evil individuals, in any way really. But in this case she is being specific to Israeli Zionists in Arab countries.

Always pay attention to Zionist. For most of the Arab world it implies a criminal act of the higest order who has not respect for human life and is essentially a racist pig with no real regard for non-Jews.

Most westerners don't understand the gravity of the Israeli issue and so can't understand this sort of desperation. [author's hi-lite]

Bad Theology

Replacement Theology

1. The Jewish people are now no longer a "chosen people." In fact, they are no different from any other group, such as the English, Spanish, or Africans.

2. Apart from repentance, the new birth, and **incorporation into the Church,** the Jewish people have no future, no hope, and no calling in the plan of God. The same is true for every other nation and group.

= First change – then God might like you! **Not true**

GRACE says 'First: accept and LOVE - Then..........

Love some more.....then

Love some more......

[in other words forget about it - they may/may not decide to change themselves: it's not your problem. You've done your part by preaching 'the word'.]

Is the New Testament anti-Semitic? Was it Intended That the Church Treat the Jewish People with Contempt?

ABSOLUTELY NOT!

While the New Testament has been used by Gentile anti-Semites, even within the Church, the writers of the New Testament were Jewish, and therefore their arguments, even critical ones, were from the vantage point of being an intra-communal debate, not inter-communal accusation. Even where the criticism is harsh, it is directed towards a particular group or sect of Jews because of their practices, which needed correcting. For example, even though Yeshua spoke harshly to the Pharisees, He nevertheless said of them, "The teachers of the law and the Pharisees sit in Moses' seat. So you must obey them and do everything they tell you. But do not do what they do, for they do not practice what they preach" (Matt: 23:2-3). He was distressed that they were "missing the mark" in their self-righteousness, which is something all of us need to be careful of doing.

The clear teaching of the New Testament is that the Church was and is to love and honour the Jewish people. In Ephesians 2:11-18, we are told that "by the blood of Messiah," we Gentiles are "made near" to the commonwealth of Israel, the covenants, promises and hopes given to Israel. In Romans 11:11-12, 25, we are told that "blindness in part" has come to the Jews so that the message would be forced out into the nations. Nevertheless, we are told that a time would come when "all Israel would be saved" (v. 26), because the gifts and callings of God towards Israel and the Jewish people were given without repentance (v. 29). God's relationship with Israel and the Jewish people is everlasting.

We Gentile Christians are told that the Jews are "beloved for the sake of the Patriarchs" (Rom. 11:28). They are a chosen people who fulfilled their calling and brought the Gospel to the world. They were chosen to:

Be obedient to God's Word and demonstrate to the world as "a light to the nations:" Hear God's Word and record it - the Bible. Be the human channel for the Messiah.

this passage clearly shows that we Gentiles are the "wild olive branches," who get our life from being grafted into the olive tree. The tree represents the covenants, promises and hopes of Israel (Eph. 2:12), rooted in the Messiah and fed by the sap, which represents the Holy Spirit, giving life to the Jews (the "natural branches") and Gentile alike. We Gentiles are told to remember that the olive tree holds us up and NOT to be arrogant or boast against the "natural branches" because they can be grafted in again. The olive tree is NOT the Church. We are simply grafted into God's plan that preceded us for over 2,000 years.

RE Levav, Kohn, Golding & Weissman Study 1997

RESULTS: While no differences were found among females, Jewish males had significantly higher rates of major depression than Catholics, Protestants, and all non-Jews combined. Jews had a 1:1 female-to-male ratio for major depression, in contrast to the other religious groups, which approached the universal 2:1 ratio. Rates of alcohol abuse /dependence were inversely related to rates of major depression. CONCLUSIONS: The results support only in part the earlier reports that **Jews have higher rates of depression**. The equal gender distribution of major depression among Jews may be associated with the lower rate of alcoholism among Jewish males.

What this is saying is that Jewish males tend to BE depressed, not try to cover it up.[Depressed people can choose either to ignore it [alcohol, drugs, fast cars/accidents, suicide are common methods of DENIAL] or 'feel their feelings'.] Jewish men **have** their feelings, rather than **deny** them or act childishly. This is by far the best choice. Drinking alcohol can [per se] cause depression by damping down brain function like a sedative drug.

Why are Jewish men depressed? Cross Currents Winter 2002/03 , Editor,33 Russell St., Toronto, Ontario M5S 2S1, tel (416) 595-6714 comments on present research e-mail hema-zbogar@camh.net.

Jewish men are sadder than most. This is not a proven scientific fact, but my personal opinion. However, this much we do know: although women in the general population are more likely to suffer from depression and anxiety than men, depression rates are essentially equal among Jewish men and women. Why so?

In 1977, after an extensive review of the literature, Dr. Myrna Weissman and Dr. Gerald Klerman confirmed that women experience depression more than men. Twenty years later, Weissman and three colleagues looked at the sex ratio for depression among Jews. They examined results from New Haven and Los Angeles, cities with large Jewish populations. Jews were identified on the basis of their response to the question: "What is your religious preference?" Of approximately 4,000 people in the study, 400 identified as Jews. The prevalence of depression among Jewish men and women was equal. There were no differences in depression rates among women, no matter what their religious affiliation. But depression rates for Jewish men were twice that for non-Jewish males

The conclusions of the 1997 study implied that lower alcohol use might explain the high incidence of depression among Jewish males. The theory is that alcohol use may mask depression. Thus, Weissman et al posited that the higher prevalence of depression among Jewish men could be attributed to the fact that Jewish men drink less than non-Jewish males. There is some support for the idea that abstinence from alcohol is correlated with high depression rates. One study by Loewenthal and colleagues, which surveyed Orthodox synagogues in the United Kingdom, found equal gender rates for depression and no alcohol dependency. A 1993 study of young adults in Israel, where rates of alcohol dependency are relatively low, also reported equal rates of depression among

Jewish women and men. And the Amish, a population that does not drink, present high rates of depression, equal in women and men.

Yet alcohol (or lack thereof) may not explain everything. Depression questionnaires rely on questions that refer to the body and perceived changes in body functions. Traditionally, these are the items that are more frequently endorsed by women than men. It has been estimated that as many as 25 per cent of women (but only eight per cent of men) can be described as hypochondriachal or extra-conscious of body symptoms. Could the "Jewish mother syndrome" explain why, among Jewish men, body sensitivity is higher?

California psychologist Dr. Susan Nolen-Hoeksema has attributed the greater susceptibility of women to depression to their more ruminative style of coping when distressed. This contrasts with what most men do, which is to become active in the face of stress. If ruminating about problems rather than distracting oneself is associated with depression, it may explain the vulnerability to depression in Jewish men, whose religious training reinforces a ruminative quest for knowledge: In much wisdom is much grief, and he that increaseth knowledge, increaseth sorrow (Eccles. 1:14).

The Canadian Network for Mood and Anxiety Treatment Depression Working Group published guidelines in 1999 stating that the prevalence of depression is similar across cultures, although the perception of depression as an illness may vary. The group warns that cultural differences may play a role in the somatization of symptoms of depression and that recent immigrants are at particular risk. Displacement, alienation and survivor guilt all likely play a role. These traits figure prominently among postwar Jews: He was oppressed and he was afflicted, yet he opened not his mouth; he is brought as a lamb to the slaughter and as a sheep before her shearers is dumb, so openeth not his mouth (Isaiah 53:7)

Still, despite socio-cultural speculations, the primary explanation for susceptibility to depression remains genetic. Why would genes for depression survive in a discrete population? What evolutionary purposes would they have served? It has been postulated that yielding and withdrawing in the face of aggression (as Jews have been forced to do throughout Biblical and more recent history), increase the likelihood of survival. Depression, as per Freud's formulation, is aggression turned inward against the self, a form of dirge and lamentation associated with Judaism from before the time of Job. In the Jewish struggle to survive for six millennia, could it be that evolution has selected for submissive depressive-prone genes?

Depression and anxiety disorders among Jews from the former Soviet Union five years after their immigration to Israel

Epidemiological studies have shown that the prevalence rates of major depression and anxiety are lower in the elderly than in younger adults, a finding consistent with the literature. However, after immigration, the reverse was found, with higher prevalence and incidence rates among elderly immigrants.

Perceptions of Suicide

Judaism focuses on the importance of valuing this life, and as such, suicide is tantamount to denying God's goodness in the world. Despite this, under extreme circumstances when there has seemed no choice but to either be killed or forced to betray their religion, Jews have committed individual suicide or mass suicide (see Masada, First French persecution of the Jews, and York Castle for examples) and as a grim reminder there is even a prayer in the Jewish liturgy for "when the knife is at the throat", that those dying "might sanctify God's Name". (i.e *Martyrdom*). These acts have received mixed responses by Jewish authorities, regarded both as examples of heroic martyrdom, whilst others state that it was wrong for them to take their own lives in anticipation of martyr-dom.

Suicide is not allowed in Islam; however, martyring oneself for Allah (during combat) is not considered the same as completing suicide. **Suicide in Islam is seen as a sign of disbelief in God**. [author's emphasis]

UN RESOLUTIONS 1947

General Assembly resolution 181, of Nov. 29, 1947: It calls for the partition of Palestine into Jewish and Arab states, with Jerusalem to be controlled by a "special international regime" to protect its holy places. The Zionist movement seeking to establish a Jewish state accepted the partition, the Arabs rejected it. The resolution was not carried out: After Israel declared its independence on May 14, 1948, war broke out pitting the embryonic state against surrounding 7 Arab states. Israel gained more land than it would have had under the partition resolution. Neither Israel nor Jordan, which controlled the divided parts of Jerusalem after the war, accepted control of the holy city by an international body.

1967

Security Council resolution 242, Nov. 22, 1967: It calls for "withdrawal of Israel armed forces from territories occupied" in the 1967 Six Day War and for "respect for and acknowledgment of the sovereignty, territorial integrity and political independence of every State in the area and their right to live in peace within secure and recognized boundaries free from threats or acts of force." The resolution was not carried out because the Arab side did not recognize Israel, and Israel refused to withdraw.

A Different View of Israel Who is 'in' the Plan? .

[And who 'out'!]

After reading Marcel Rebiai's book, I went to google the author and was immediately connected with a plethora of religious organisations in Jerusalem that are concerned with reconciliation [of Jews, Palestinians and Christians] which have the not inconsiderable backing and support of the American evangelical church. Having already had certain misgivings about the depth of American [Jewish and otherwise] political support for the Israelis in their struggle to subdue Palestinian protest and peacefully occupy the land, I had found Rebiai's book to be 'more of the same'. It took a three-sided conflict, then proceeded to solve it by bringing two of the combatants closer together, while completely ignoring the third party. The plan consisted of getting Christians to encourage the Jews to become Christians [or 'completed' Jews by accepting Jeshua as Messiah] which shouldn't be too difficult as the two groups share the Abramic covenant, the Old Testament scripture and the concept of the Messiah. But apart from preaching the Gospel to them I'm not sure what the plan involved, on the *Muslim* flank of the battlefield. Having given Islam the thumbs-down early in the book, the final chapter had no mention of the Muslims at all.

I couldn't help wondering why the so-extensive barrage of evangelical religious activity based in Jerusalem had not already converted the whole of the middle east over the past sixteen years of operation, and I thought about all the Bibles on the production line in the Soviet Union during the cold war – the Bibles in the factory that the tourists would see, that were just about to be published. Yes, there were Bibles being printed, but no Bibles actually achieved publication or sales, ever. Then there was the Hebrew University that hosts important international seminars about reconciliation; it certainly l*ooks* like Israelis are doing the right sorts of things [they are actually teaching Harvard and others how to do it] but nothing actually eventuates from the production line.

Then I thought of an English relative of mine who always has her TV turned on to the DIY program channel. Her house has never been renovated, re-wired, painted, papered or otherwise altered in the past fifteen years, but according to the TV programs best patronised, you would get the impression that my relative has a burning passion for the subject. What do these scenarios have in common? Lots of organisation activity and visual evidence [lots of pretence?] and no results. "If folk see all this, they will think that something is being done and they won't bother me or ask difficult questions." This way I can be a good hostess, stay polite and on good terms with the visitors, and no-one will guess that I have absolutely no intention of doing anything to change the status quo. Couple this with a quick burst of construction from time to time in the city, when no-one's looking – and Bob's your uncle.

Passive aggression. When somebody is telling you what you *ought* to do, and you don't want to do it. And you wish they would go away. [But they *don't*. They think they are helping.]

So you shrug your shoulders and say – "what can I do?" [My hands are tied. I am stuck.]

Your excuse for not making a decision, not doing anything, becomes:

"I can't! *They* are doing all the thinking for me"

[when the true self-assessment is "I can't because I have no experience in making good decisions. I am afraid I will do the wrong thing. Give away too much."]

While Israel is protected she will think, speak and behave like a victim, i.e. from a mis-judged position of over-rated entitlement. From Inside this perception, she does not have the concept of equal partners at the mediating table. Because of her history as a battered wife [anti-semitism] she always sees herself as the one with the biggest need and largest entitlement [= owed the largest concessions.] Only when the helpers GO HOME will she be able to re-assess her position, her worth more realistically with reference to the other complainant. She would like to say "Remove yourselves to the desert and stop pressurising me" to the well-meaning Christian evangelicals. But then she would have to start thinking about mediation, and she doesn't want to.

Hence the status quo.

Don't get me wrong. I am not saying anything bad about Christianity, Americans, Jews, Muslims, Jerusalem's inhabitants or anyone else. I am not on any particular 'side'. I am on everybody's side as God expects me to be. From a background well versed in group dynamics, I can see that a plan that requires a certain action on the part of each complainant to which they are averse historically [i.e.conversion] and takes into consideration the hopes and needs of only ONE of the complainants [the Jews] is de facto just as bad as replacement theology. Presumably the logic is 'If there were no promises to the Muslims in the first place, then they cannot be said to be 'replaced' if they end up with nothing.

I am not buying this, and neither should anyone else. It is grossly unfair, no matter how it is dressed up in ecclesiastical language.

The pre-requisite for mediation is the situation in which each member [complainant] starts from **the position he now occupies** – as he is *now*, where he is at *now* , being accepted at the table in his *own* skin, in his *own* clothes, in his *own* culture, in his *own* religion, as an equal person in his own right. It is no good saying 'when he is converted he will make a very nice neighbour.' The Jewish Israelis [and Hamas] must decide once and for all whether they TRUST God to do a good deal, and bring glory to himself. If they do, they should get on with the job. Get rid of the hangers-on and start the business in earnest.

I share Marcel Rebiai's enthusiasm for Jesus/Jeshua – I really do. But I can accept that there are lots of folk in the world who for various reasons belong to other faiths. I can *accept* that! It isn't a source of regret to me – it's a reason for rejoicing at the diversity of the world's creatures. If any Israeli Jews or Muslims want to accept Jeshua/Isa in a new paradigm at some time later – 'down the track' of this process of reconciliation, it will be fine. But They Don't Have To. It shouldn't be an *assumed* part of the plan. The mediation plan must start and finish as a process between Jews and Muslims.

Part of the healing is complete acceptance of the Jews themselves – as they are. Since part of their problem [unhappiness] is lack of self-acceptance and dissatisfaction, the way to curing it can not be an attitude that sees them as cannon-fodder for evangelical appeal. Recent research shows that the basic incidence of depression for Jews is twice the rate in the non-Jewish population, and that the rate for men equals the rate for women. [Normally women have double the rate compared with men.] And as mentioned elsewhere, the personality structure in the east is more akin to that of the Arabs than it is in the west. Lets see where this takes us.

In evolutionary terms, if a characteristic is enhanced in a population it must have a long-term benefit, or it would have been dropped. Genes have to be protective, enhance total 'fitness' and success for the clan. Depression works because it renders unhappy/unproductive individuals very quiet and ignor-able leaving the rest of the clan free to go about the normal work of daily survival. Un-depressed people usually react angrily/violently when they disagree, but the depressed person is quiet and withdrawn into himself. From the point of view of the clan's relationship with the outside world; the rest of the world doesn't like depressed people, so it avoids them. Being with them makes you feel miserable, it's as though the heavy weight of gloom is infectious, you feel yourself being pulled down. They are not responsive, no fun to be with. So they are either passed by [because they are doing their 'solitude' thing,] or in company they are avoided.

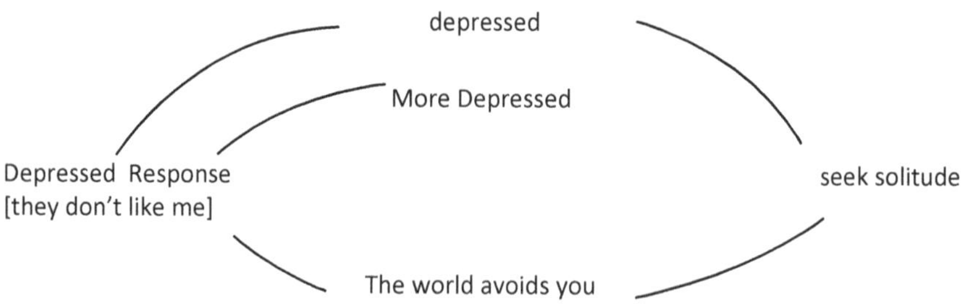

The long-term net-result is that it's *good* for the world that the Jews are quiet, depressed, sitting in solitude and mourning. We can ignore them [or punish them when they get too frisky and start being successful.] But is that *what the* **Jews** *want to happen* – now and for ever?

I think not. The problem is, when non-assertive individuals start to turn their lives around, their impatience often makes them over-compensate at first and become demanding and aggressive – instead of assertive. That can be a worry, because there is a **lot of anger** from the past that can come out and **crush by-standers**, inadvertently. So there is a need for 'gently, gently' [i.e. a lot of self-control] while things are settling down.

The Combatants

We have two originally Semitic peoples who are competing for the same 'land of their fathers.'

God covenanted with Abraham the Patriarch – he was promised land, seed and blessing. Secondly this future 'people' would be a blessing to the whole world. [That was the point of the whole exercise.]

The first part has come true already. But the 'blessing to the whole world' has been more or less dragged out of Israel without their consent. [Fair enough. If I were a specially chosen child, I doubt I would want to share my fortune with other children.] But it happened anyway.

From Jesus onwards, the Jewish blessings became shared with the Christian church. Secondly [just as instructed in the gospel parable] Mohammed hammered on the door of the Jews [in Medina] and asked for some bread. *But they wouldn't open the door to him, and they didn't throw the bread out of the window either. This wasn't the first time they had been refused, it followed the pattern set when Hagar and Ishmael were thrown out of Abraham's household.

So this opportunity to put things right *went unrecognised* by the Jews approached in Medina. Now we switch to 2010 and we have the third instance of rejection. Israel is back in the promised land, and nothing has changed. Rebiai says p62

'everything that precedes – the history of Israel and the nations – is broken and pruned, ' [i.e.when the Messiah comes.]

But Jesus *doesn't come to break people down*. [Jews, Muslims or anyone else.] He comes to build people up. If individual Jews /Muslims WANT to receive Jesus and enter his kingdom that would be absolutely wonderful, but it has to be voluntary.] Likewise on p63 Marcel says 'the branches of Ishmael must be broken out of their history, culture and tradition, out of their ethnic and national circumstances. Like the rest of humanity they must be broken....' [and led back through the Messiah]

Sounds very painful to me, and we should not wish it on anyone. That's not the Messiah that I know, who gave his life "when we were yet sinners". If we are talking about whether or not we *deserve* what God is wanting to give us, we know that *no-one* does. It can only be taken up voluntarily by someone brought to that position by the Holy Spirit.

On p65 Rebiai shows us Isaiah's prophecy; - release of blessing for the whole world when the sons of Abraham are reconciled to each other. Isaiah 19:24-25. What a great day that will be! And it's not far away! But it will not come by forcing Messiah[Jesus] on everyone.

He thinks p66 that the 'weapon of darkness' is Islam [because it rejects the Jews,] but the Jewish rejection of Muslims came first. It is easy to recognise the explicit language of rejection in the Koran, but the best disguise of the devil is to appear modern and civilised; sophisticated global citizens [with the considerable benefit of a century's long opportunity for assimilation]. Just as the rich western Jews were embarrassed by the less educated cash-strapped eastern European relatives, so they are dismissive of the peasants/barbarians who are the indigenous inhabitants of Palestine. Otherwise why would innocent middle-aged shepherds be attacked and beaten by Israeli youths? [Fair sport – they don't count. They're not actually *people*.] The Canadian women's photographic work at the check-points records many such incidents as part of 'normal' every-day life.

We are reminded on p67 that the Muslims will not get anywhere until they renounce hatred, enmity and violence. This is quite true. But it also applies to the Jews. *Because* it's inside their heads and not displayed by such vehement language [and terrorist costume] it is easier to pretend it isn't there. [See p13 – passive aggression] In fact the Muslim Palestinians have come a long way in a short time and are now able to peacefully demonstrate their nationalism to the community [local and global] as a paramilitary group, finishing up their marching demonstration by lying on the ground to show their peaceful intentions. I don't think the Jewish Israelis have made *anything like* the same progress in attitude in the corresponding timespan. Their commando style approach to all situations – from the boat going to Gaza, to the capture of their soldier on the Lebanese border – indicates the concrete immutability of their style.

*Mohammed knocking on the door of the Jews in Medina

Compare Matt.7: 7-12

Family Counselling View of the Conflict

One might conceptualise the family as comprising mother and father [Land and God] and six children; in order of seniority these would be

Adopted Muslims	1300yrs old	[Ottoman up till 1917]
Orthodox Jews	135yrs old	[since 1875 – Mea Shearim]
Zionists	90yrs old	[fighting Arabs/X'ns since 1917]
Holocaust victims	75yrs old	[Nazi purge since 1935 onwards]
Military	45yrs	[in a central position since 1967]
Secular moderates	40 yrs old	influx followed nation-hood

The parents have a stormy relationship with multiple separations and re-unions. At present they are divorced.

Personal Characters of the Children

Orthodox – passionately **FOR God** – [but not for land/Israel - not lawful]

Zionist – passionately **FOR Land** [try to avoid God's opinion altogether]

Holocaust victims – came to grief because they had **no homeland**

Military – ostensibly **hates Muslims**

Muslims – **hate their step-brothers**, but love their parents [God & Land]

Secular Moderates –only weakly pro-god, pro-land; **strong sense justice**

How does **each child** describe **the problem?**

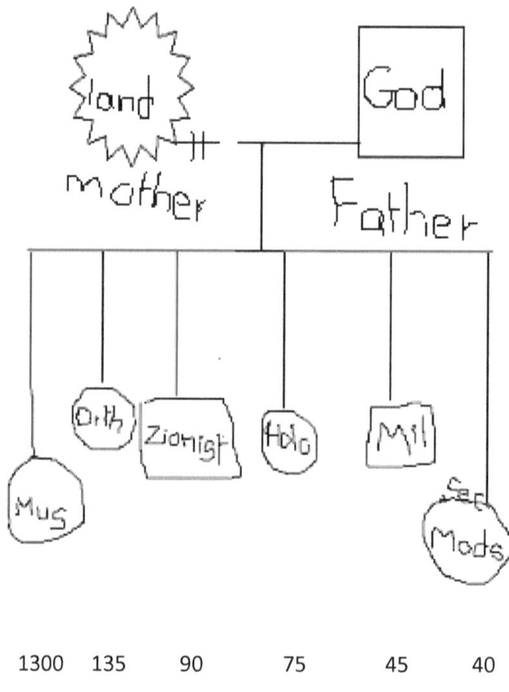

What is the problem?

O –“ Secular govt. has put itself above God – taken the land without His guidance & permission That’s why it’s all a disaster.”

Z – “Religious quibbles hold us back from doing what is obviously right. The land was promised us in ancient times. We’re entitled to live here.” [Muslims should leave and go to Arabic countries where they belong.]

Holocaust Victims – “if you don’t have your own country you’re not safe.”

Mil’ary – “bastard Muslims are unpredictable. Security is hard to get”

Adopted **Mus**lims –“ We have been here for 1300yrs, now Zionists want to throw us out of our own country.” [We are treated like scum]

Secular **mod**erates – there is no sense of unity. Every faction is out for itself, nobody cares about the other guy – especially the Muslims. I'd like to bang their heads together – maybe get some sense out of them.

How They Interact

Orthodox are poor, pacifist, defensive. Obsessively interested in the **Law** /Obedience. **'Only with God's permission** do we take the land.' Therefore, secular Israel is blasphemous. [Acting on their own will, not God's] Orthodox are very 'black or white' – there is no grey.

The majority of **Muslims** are also defenceless, live in refugee compounds, have **no** capital city /government buildings/army /shops & community facilities; **poor** education and work prospects. Their land and houses are expropriated at will by the Jewish Israelis. They are **treated worse than slaves**, with an attitude of **contempt**. We could say they have been **stripped naked** of all resources, like the Jews before they entered the gas ovens of Auswitchz.

Holocaust victims are dead, but **very powerful forces** in the daily life of the country. They represent 3-4 generations of mourning relatives, in those extended families which have survived. The psychological effect on the now-living is tremendous.

The two 'offensive' [rather than defensive] siblings are the Zionists and the Military. The **Zionist** position is "take it while you can" [the end justifies any means; their **nationalism over-rides** any other consideration.] Since Land and God have parted company, you can't be strongly devoted to both at the same time without being schizophrenic, so the **Zionists** choose to **stay with Land** and 'let God go.'

The **Military** have most **influence on the youth**. They **generally hate everyone, including themselves** – this is the effect that having to oppress others on a daily basis has on them. It is difficult to justify acting immorally, so they cope through a system of denial. They hate Muslims, Orthodox Religious, Holocaust victims and weakness of any kind. They hate to show feelings [=being a woman] and measure their personal success in terms of assertiveness and physical strength. They are certain that the whole world is against them, and they must never betray any signs of weakness or compassion.

In a desperate attempt to rise above the WW2 events in an action-replay, they refuse to be the victims – in doing so they become the strong tormentors. They despise the victims of genocide for being so helpless and vulnerable. [Last-mentioned souls being their own grand - parents and great-grand-parents, they identify only too easily with these people and their fate, and it is very uncomfortable.]

Because their fate was related to their strange clothes and customs, as well as their idio-syncratic relationship with God, this makes the strong beliefs and odd appearance of the Orthodox unacceptable. They would become useful objects of ridicule and the butt of jokes about mediaeval culture and archaic ritual [somewhat unpatriotic?] were it not for the fact that Muslims offer a better more responsive, convenient target. Orthodox Jews have no sense of humour and are too passive, whereas the Muslims are more spunky and inclined to retaliate aggressively when provoked. They are more fun to annoy, and there is permission.

Orthodox Jews and Muslims have many features in common : strange clothes and insistence on covering the body, strange habits [wailing, bowing down to the ground to pray,] strange food preferences, strange rituals performed on festive occasions, obsessive habits to do with cleanliness and public health [given when germs and antibiotics were unknown.] One makes a good substitute for the other, if you need to act out your anger and remain patriotic at the same time.

The discipline and formality of the army encourages the attitudes of strength and intolerance to wimps, that characterise the bully. The opportunity to re-enact WW2 bullying –this time in the position of the winner, not the loser – actually works for some, but is extremely distressing for others of a softer nature. There are of course many more ingenious and creative ways of grieving [= annihilating one's embarrassing past] hitherto unexplored, that await discovery....

While all this is going on, there are many individuals who are working hard to bring in real democracy, trying to correct injustices, counter racial hatred, model equality and sharing rather than selfishness and greed, and above all - bring peace. This is the **REAL remnant of the faithful**. They don't *look* religious, they don't necessarily *belong* to activist groups, they just *recognise the difference* between fairness and justice [on one hand] and the inhuman treatment of fellow human beings on the other, and are **willing to say/do something** about it. Generally [not always] younger, they are not as tied to the past, to history and traditions, and are therefore more free in attitudes and perceived options. But apart from being exasperated at times, they do not ridicule those individuals who **are** [connected with the past.] Sometimes [not always] they are more widely educated in the ways of the world, and can relate to other nationalities more easily. They reject the more extreme dismissive/cruel attitudes of Zionists and Military, and wish to be PRO-ACTIVE towards the future rather than RE-active towards the past. Only weakly attached to Mother and Father [LAND & GOD] in spirit rather than in substance, they are balanced and motivated enough to honour the Covenant, and equipped to bring it about. Their's is the responsibility to *hear* the good spirit's prompting, and set it in motion.

Terry Fullam used to say "if God can speak through Balaam's ass!......" He can speak through anybody.

Some principles to ponder/research:

Adopted children vs legitimate children – rights & obligations

Will claimants; whether folk who turn up claiming parentage should be allowed a share? – and how much? [both have Abraham's DNA].

Parable of the Prodigal Son – one coming back after a long absence vs the one who stayed home & did all the work on the land for his father.

The question of someone caring for your stuff after a disaster – should the response be "keep right out of **my** place" or "thanks for caring in my absence" [i.e.'the Rock' and the Dome of the Rock] See bottom p55

Something else to ponder:

Might it be possible that the 'security/security/security' theme could be a smoke-screen that serves the purpose by making the Muslims out to be the bad guys, when in fact the problem is civil unrest amongst the grass-roots population?

If so – there is HOPE – something can be done to effect change.

How the Family Metaphor Helps

One past characteristic of the Jewish nation was its strong solidarity based on the Old covenant identity. An individual Jew knew who he was – he belonged to the Nation of Israel's children. He was promised to God from birth, to do his will in the world so that eventually the Nation would be great; blessed by God with many descendants, Israel would be used by God to be a blessing to the whole world.

With a destiny as enormously important as that, you might be forgiven for occasionally getting off track, and failing in your duty. That is a truly overwhelming objective, a once-and-for-all eternally binding obligation, or contract; made between God and Abraham in pre-history. At first the early history of the tribes was transmitted orally in stories and songs and poetry, later on it was written down as the Pentateuch and included the all-important Law of Moses.

From the beginning the seeds of the Arabic races were there, in the shape of Ishmael, the eldest son of Abraham, who was borne by Sarah's maid [Abraham's concubine.] Abraham couldn't believe that Sarah would have a baby when God promised them a child - she was too old, so Abraham helped things along as best as he could. Hagar and Ishmael dutifully disappeared into the desert and it wasn't until nearly 700yrs later that the descendants turned up and demanded their portion of the family fortune.

To give him his due, Mohammed *asked the Jews politely* to accept him and Ishmael's descendants as brothers [or at least, step-brothers.] But they were refused, and they ridiculed Mohammed's suggested contribution to the Law. Just like an unknown impostor turning up at the solicitor's, waving an obscure piece of paper purporting to be the last will of the deceased, he was laughed out of town and designated "illegal", fraudulent, avaricious and all the things said of the fortune hunter wanting to steal the rightful inheritance of the **real** inheritors.

Another place that the Covenant-inheritors went wrong, was to be so desperate to get back into their promised Land that they took it by force, instead of waiting for general consensus. It is understandable that people who had witnessed the WW2 Holocaust would be so anxious to find safety as soon as possible, but the urgency was *not quite* of a nature that required immediate rescue. It was more of a psychological anxiety than an emergency physical safety issue. It did not warrant just *any* action, regardless of consequences. The consequences have indeed been disastrous. Instead of the tightly-knit inter-dependent extended family-clan system, there is now civil dissention between several [would-be sibling] factions. This is because the greatest factor that united them [right from their creation as a potential Nation 2,000yrs BC] the Covenant of Abraham, has now become the symbol of disagreement and disunity.

To recover a functioning Nation, the separate factions must be united again under the Old Covenant – the LAND mother and the father GOD must be understood once more to be one -in the light of the first agreement; Genesis chapter 12. When the children of Israel return to their Covenant obligations, all will be well.

In a true democracy, the people should be able to express their wills clearly to their government, when it becomes obvious that they have the answer to problems that their government is not handling well. To be able to meet, discuss, deliberate and report back to Knesset, is one option for breaking the impass that beleaguers Israel at the moment. Such a possibility exists, and has already been used with success in Australia and USA obtaining new ideas at grass-roots level for an identified problem in a difficult socially disruptive scenario. It is called IDA. http://www.onlineopinion.com.au/view.asp?article=1057

The [Full] Process

Rebiai on p68 gives his outline of the process – the order in which the various groups will be reconciled.

I have already disagreed with the underlying assumption that all the reconciliation will be the result of conversion to the Messianic scheme, with Jesus as Messiah - in other words, conversion to Christianity - which is either an imposition [if enforced] or unrealistic [if expected as some sort of dramatic sweeping world-wide movement.]

I also disagree with the order which is laid out. In therapy we generally move from the easiest to the hardest, of the list of things we want to achieve. That way the little successes build on each other so as to increase hope and expectancy for the future. The hope and expectancy grows **faith** – which is the *choice* to believe something CAN be achieved, and the *willingness* to put something solid of yourself 'on the table.'

Marcel puts Jews & Jews first, Jews & Arabs second, and Arabs & Arabs last. As I see it, the Jews are the **most damaged** emotionally, as the *Holocaust* of WW2 is still fresh, and the *disappointment* of realising that they weren't 'restored' in a practical way is current, NOW. [In comparison, the state of affairs for Muslims is much the same as it ever was – rejection by the Jews. It's not a surprise or fresh disappointment.]

I see the strongest **connection** as being between the Arabs *inside* Israel and the Arabs *outside*. This is also affirmed by the fact that it is *Jordanian* leaders who have taken the initiative to use the UN for an interfaith statement of peace. So this is step 1, and it is already happening.

Step 2 is chapter 9 Page 51 – the coming together of the Jews themselves, in democratic deliberation to ascertain what they themselves think about what is possible and what is out of the question. [Without any prompting from would-be 'helpers.'] Obviously there are liberal hope-ful Jews, & fundamentalist narrow Jews who find it difficult to change. They would all have to put their case to one another, *trusting that God* would put a spirit of acceptance and *tenderness* in the hearts of their colleagues. They would need to find a way to re-unite the 'divorced parents' Land & God [=restore the Covenant Relationship.] They would need to agree that they were on the **threshold of a New Era** – one **which liberated their youth** to build for the future [by first acknowledging, then letting go of the past.] All this is possible.[See IDA]

Step 3 would be the Peace Process itself; reconciling of Muslims and Jews. All Muslims would have to **recognise Israel**, [including Hamas, there is no alternative to sharing.] So would the Orthodox Jews who don't accept Israel unless God is in Charge. The Jews would have to **recognise the rights** of Palestinians [to be treated as equal partners at the mediating table] as arising unconditionally, inherent with life itself, unrelated to culture/history or any other bad memories in the past. Everyone would have to be committed to the joint future.

<u>What Jews/Muslims need </u>from each other. Forgiveness.

Jews need to say "Sorry"

We excluded you from the promises.

1. When Hagar & Ishmael were rejected from the household
2. When Mohammed 'knocked & asked us for bread' [Medina]
3. When we assumed ourselves to be sole inheritors [Palestine]

Muslims need to say "Sorry"

We responded with hate and violence.

1. When we treated you ill, as 2nd-class citizens in Islamic countries
2. When we feared for our survival & identity, forming militias
3. When we used terrorism against innocent unsuspecting members of the public to get attention

Respective Needs

It is more important for the Muslims to keep a *firm grasp of the old*, for the sake of their identity. Unless their connection with the past is firm, they will not be able to leave it behind and create a new identity. To help them move into the 21st Century with confidence, they will need to reassert their ownership of Land and holy places.

It is more important for the Jews to *mourn for the holocaust* and get it out of their system so they can move forward. The *young folk need permission* to let the bad memories go, which allows them scope to use their imagination /strength to build a new future.

Practical Issues – The Old & the New

There is only one Jerusalem. A fertile imagination will be the pre-requisite to accommodating everyone. There is only one Temple Mount, and there is no existing [historic] Jewish Temple as such, apart from the remaining Herodian foundation known as the 'wailing wall'. Immediately after the six-day war, the Moroccan quarter round the Wailing Wall was blown up, to clear a space for worship; [no-one knows whether their occupants were re-housed, or where.] Cleared of houses it became a big sterile empty white-paved area.

On the other side of the wall is the Dome of the Rock. The Muslims call this sacred ground where the temple once stood "Haram as-Sharif" the Noble Sanctuary – no house has ever intruded here, although it is 2/3 the size of the Old cramped Muslim area [1/6 of the entire Old City.] Looking at the golden Dome of the Rock, the Muslim is reminded of what he once was – master of half the known world, confident in Allah's beneficence. This magnificent building shields the all-important bare 'rock' that marks the site of the altar in Solomon's Temple.

'In the time of Abd al-Malik, the builder of the shrine, the Rock was bathed every Monday and Thursday in saffron, ambergris, rosewater and musk. Silk curtains were drawn around it, while servants with scented hands and feet walked over it in procession, carrying gold and silver censers.' Colin Thubron FRSL, 'Jerusalem'Time-Life 1976

Nothing was too extravagant for the site where Abraham demonstrated his devotion to God by preparing to sacrifice his son, only to be told that an animal should be offered in his stead. The story of anointing the Rock with perfumes reminds me of the Matt.26; 6-13 story where the woman in Bethany anointed Jesus, and was scolded for wasting money.

The most sacred site, in **the** most sacred city, thus supports two complete Muslim buildings, [Dome of the Rock and Al Aqsa Mosque] & a second [ruined] portion of Solomon/Herod's Temple which is the only part left in its original state and not enclosed/protected/adorned or in any way 'claimed' by the Muslims. Surrounding these three items are large expanses of 'holy' covered ground that cannot be used for any other purpose. The Rock is important to **both** Muslims **and** Jews.

The old story to illustrate the wisdom of Solomon involved cutting the disputed child in two, so the two sets of parents could each have a bit. We could use the same sort of wisdom here; or we could call it 'tooth-paste wisdom.' If one partner hates the way the other partner squeez-es from the middle [instead of the bottom, carefully rolling up the metal] the thing to do is provide each partner with his own tube!

The answer – provide two articles, [temples] one Jewish, one Muslim.

The Al Aksa Mosque was built on land desecrated with dung – that's how important it was for them to have it. [As we all know, Muslims hate filth!] So it seems practical to allow the Muslims to have charge of their own building. Since land is at a premium on the mount, and Israel would need a **very big** temple if they were to build a new one, perhaps they could take an idea from Genesis 12 "then Abram built an altar there [at Shekem] to the Lord, who had appeared to him." Every time some important exchange had gone on, the Patriarchs would build an altar to mark the occasion. [At the transfiguration of Jesus, Peter asked should he build *three tents* or tabernacles for them - Moses, Elijah and Jesus].

So perhaps Israel could build a *small but highly significant remembrance* of Solomon's Temple on the important sacred site; the space needed would be minimal – the size perhaps of a generous broom-cupboard. Enough to describe and explain Solomon's Temple and the short-lived temple built by Herod the Great on the same site. The historical development might be included: first the simple stone altar, then the [mobile] Ark of the Covenant and the Tent, for the desert wanderings, then the special building envisaged by David, fixed in one place opposite his Capital City.

If a New Era Temple were to be built by the Jews it could signify the difference between animal sacrifices of the ancestors and the personal inward sacrifice that we understand to be requested of us today. This new [era] modern Temple could be built in a residential area – so as to bring the temple to the people, rather than the *People to the Temple.*

These two new sites would be statements -of the old and the new; the past and the future. By giving past history pride of place, Israel has :

1. An [albeit smaller] *tribute to her long history* with Yahweh, and a focal end-point for historical processions.
2. a *symbol of ownership* of The Mount, as a sacred site.
3. *the practical needs of the people* addressed with a *strong future emphasis.*

If allowed, the young people [and the Muslims] could teach Israeli Jews how to *diminish* the size of the 'mourning' temple-motif in their minds and hearts and *increase* the size of the 'hopeful/new' temple-motif. After all, it has been the Assyrians and Romans who have insisted on obliterating it, not the Muslims.

They would still share the Rock with the Muslims, and still have the Wailing Wall to themselves – if they felt an overwhelming need to wail, from time to time. [Hopefully less often, as time went on.]

With this scheme, Muslims and Jews each have one shared item [Rock]; Jews have one exclusive Wailing Wall, one exclusive New Temple, one exclusive *symbol* of antiquity on Mount Moriah [other than the Rock and the Wall.] The Muslims have one exclusive mosque [Aqsa] and one shared mosque which is the equivalent of Solomon's Temple in beauty and materials; the Dome of the Rock. Both complete buildings are testimony to 1300 years of Muslim residence.

Strange to think that the only Temple Jesus would have been familiar with was the strange Romanesque one that Herod built. There were no golden domes in those days.

New Administration of Sacred Buildings [Temple Mount in particular]

It might be a workable plan to alternate admin between the two parties, in the same way that competing political parties exchange leadership on a regular basis in a democracy. For example, Muslims could do three years, then the Jews three years, then every seventh year could be international so as to allow Christians, Buddhists and others of an interfaith persuasion greater access and imaginative use, as well as the opportunity to serve in some way.

FAQ - Democratic Deliberation

Please see Wikipedia IDA Australia/America, or link on page 51

This is a system devised by a psychologist/ political scientist Pamela Ryan which allows a representational cross-section of the population to 'DO iTS DUTY' for the country, by deliberating on the particular social issue that has become problematical. Just as a 12-man jury is expected to represent the wider community in judging one of its peers, so does the 400-strong deliberation group hunker down to thrash out the problems of the day on behalf of their community. Results can not be guessed before the end of the process – sometimes they are surprising.

The 'mini'population must of course be completely representative, containing all members residing in the land – no-one is excluded. The facilitators likewise must be as impartial as judges are at court, and there must be a good selection of experts and information-givers on hand to give a true and accurate account of the factors involved – from diverse backgrounds such as religious, social science, demographics mental health.

Bibliography

Vulnerability of Jews to affective disorders
I Levav, R Kohn, JM Golding and MM Weissman
Department of Psychiatry and Human Behavior, Brown University, Providence, RI 02906, USA.

Depression and Demoralization Among Russian-Jewish Immigrants in Primary Care
Zinoviy Gutkovich M.D, Richard N. Rosenthal M.D, Igor Galynker M.D. Ph.D., Christopher Muran, Ph.D., Sarai Batchelder, Ph.D., and Elena Itskhoki, M.D.

Re page 33; see Psychosomatics 40:117-125, April 1999
© 1999 The Academy of Psychosomatic Medicine
Zilber, N., Lerner, Y., Eidelman, R. and Kertes, J. (2001), Depression and anxiety disorders among Jews from the former Soviet Union five years after their immigration to Israel. International Journal of Geriatric Psychiatry, 16: 993–999.doi: 10.1002/gps.456

Re p 31 Article Winter 2002-3 Ed'n **Cross Currents** Journal [Canadian Mental Health]
High rate Jewish Male Depression, v low rate alcohol abuse; with editor's permission
Re p 29 Is the NT Anti-semitic? "**Bridges for Peace**", *May 9, 2002 edit'n*
AustralianFilm **SHINE** David Helfgott's story, 1st gen.after survivor of Auschwitz

Islam, Israel and the Church **Marcel Rebiai**, Sovereign World 2006

Raphael Patai 1910-1996, **Hungary, Palestine '33 & USA '52**
Inside the Jewish Mind, [1977] Scribner N.Y.Rev.Edit'n 1996
Inside the Arab Mind, [1976] Scribner N.Y. Rev. Edit'n 2002

www.btselem.org **for info on 'separation fence' [racial segregation wall]**

Construction Progress [as of August 2009]

	Length (Km)	Percentage of barrier's length
Completed construction	409	56.6
Under construction	73	10.2
Construction not yet begun	223	31.5
Total	709	100

www.ingramcontent.com/pod-product-compliance
Ingram Content Group UK Ltd.
Pitfield, Milton Keynes, MK11 3LW, UK
UKHW041839200726
13854UKWH00003BA/1227

9 781446 625231